THE STORY OF
OXFORD

A short history of the City of Oxford, as seen in the displays and collections of the Museum of Oxford, St Aldates, Oxford

ALAN SUTTON

First published in the United Kingdom in 1992
Alan Sutton Publishing Ltd · Phoenix Mill · Far Thrupp · Stroud · Gloucestershire

Oxfordshire Books · Oxfordshire County Council · Leisure and Arts
Central Library · Westgate · Oxford

British Library Cataloguing in Publication Data

Oxfordshire County Council
  Story of Oxford
  I. Title
  942.574

  ISBN 0–7509–0097–0

Typeset in 10/12 Palatino.
Typesetting and origination by
Alan Sutton Publishing Limited.
Colour separation by Yeo Graphics
  Reproductions Ltd.
Printed in Great Britain by
The Bath Press, Bath, Avon.

Port Meadow by J.A. Shuffrey (1859–1939), showing Lower Wolvercote and St Peter's church. Port Meadow, Oxford's 'common' from Saxon times, has been untouched by ploughing for over a thousand years

The Setting

The River Cherwell joins the Thames at Oxford where the town was first established on low-lying ground at the tip of a gravel terrace between the two rivers. The upper layer of gravel had been carried down river from the Cotswold area during warm intervals between the Ice Ages, about a quarter of a million years ago. The hills through which the Thames flows below Oxford are much older, composed of limestone and clay, formed when the area was covered by sea. The sediments, including the remains of sea creatures, became the rocks and fossils of today. The rivers continued to dictate Oxford's development, for as the town spread beyond the gravel terrace, the city centre and North Oxford were separated from East, West and South Oxford by the rivers and adjacent floodable meadows, which for a long time delayed building development. The central area retains much open space, with large college and private gardens, playing fields and parks. Port

Meadow and the river meadows near Holywell, Magdalen College and Iffley provide a habitat for waterfowl. The snakeshead fritillary flourishes in Magdalen Meadow and at Iffley. Patches of ancient forest are preserved on the hills close to the city, at Shotover, Wytham and Bagley. In East Oxford Bullingdon Bog has peat deposits containing orchids and other rare species.

Prehistoric Times

The Thames valley gravels were a major area of settlement in prehistoric times, and near Oxford the floodplain was then much drier, allowing settlement, for example, on Port Meadow. Early stone tools have been found at St Ebbe's and Wolvercote, and there are signs of a neolithic settlement near Christ Church. Bronze Age barrows have been identified on Port Meadow, a linear barrow cemetery in the University Parks, and a double-ditched barrow in the nearby Science Area. A settlement of the Beaker period has been found in St Thomas Street. In the Iron Age, heavy occupation of Port Meadow is suggested by ring ditches and enclosures, and undated sites of similar character are visible from the air in the University Parks and South Oxford (on the former Oxford City football ground).

Two arrowheads hand-chipped from flint in the neolithic period (New Stone Age), found in Christ Church Meadow and the University Parks
By courtesy of Dr E.J. Bowen and the Ashmolean Museum

Handmade pottery beaker dug up in Summertown. Such beakers were fashionable drinking vessels in the late neolithic period, and it was a sign of prestige to be buried with one
By courtesy of the Ashmolean Museum

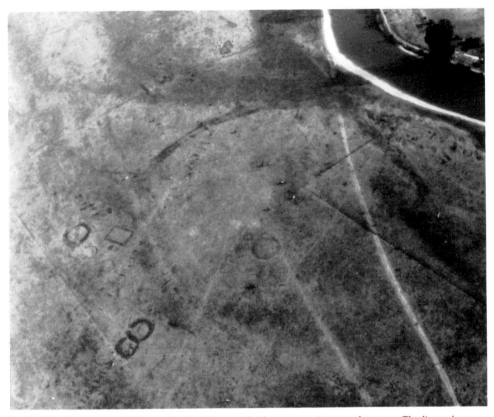

In Port Meadow traces of Bronze Age burial mounds show up as rings on the grass. The linear features may be Iron Age farms and boundaries

By courtesy of the Committee for Aerial Photography, University of Cambridge

Potteries and Roman Highways

The Roman invaders did not build a town on the site of Oxford, but there are signs of settlements in North Oxford, probably strung out along a north–south road which roughly followed the line of the modern Banbury Road. This road crossed the floodplain at North Hinksey and continued south-westwards towards a town now known to have stood at Frilford. Another road, crossing the floodplain south of Oxford, near Donnington Bridge, linked this north–south road with Roman settlements in East Oxford and Headington where many pottery kilns have been excavated, notably on the Churchill Hospital site. By the third and fourth centuries *mortaria* and luxury wares from these potteries were sold throughout Roman Britain, and pots from the Oxford area have been found in Scotland, Paris and Bruges.

Romano-British pottery kiln excavated near the Churchill hospital with *mortaria* (mixing bowls) from the same site. The kiln dates from the late third or early fourth century AD

Fragment of a mortar from the Churchill site, scratched before firing with the potter's name: TAMESIBUGUS FECIT ('Thames dweller made it')

The Coming of the Saxons

In the late fourth and early fifth centuries the Roman occupation ended and Saxon invaders penetrated the Thames valley. By AD 635 St Birinus was established as bishop at Dorchester, eight miles south of Oxford, and the area was converted to Christianity. At that time there seems to have been little or no settlement on the site of Oxford, which probably formed an outlying part of a large royal estate centred on Headington.

St Frideswide and the Beginnings of Oxford

Since the Thames formed a frontier between two Anglo-Saxon kingdoms, Wessex and Mercia, a habitable site at an established crossing place was likely to become important. Of Mercian Oxford, however, almost nothing is known, yet by the early tenth century the site was occupied by a major town.

Tradition links the beginnings of Oxford with St Frideswide, part of whose legend, first recorded in the twelfth century, depicts her as a pious Mercian princess who became a nun in an Oxford monastery founded at her behest; she was pestered by a lecherous royal suitor who was struck blind when he tried to enter Oxford to seize her, but he recovered at Frideswide's intercession, and she continued in the monastery until her death. Scholars now think that Frideswide was a real person associated with Oxford and nearby Binsey, and that a religious house, perhaps for a mixed community of monks and nuns, with Frideswide as first abbess, was indeed founded about AD 700 on the site of Christ Church. It was burned down in AD 1002, rebuilt, and in AD 1122 refounded as the Augustinian priory of St Frideswide. A cemetery, probably attached to the first St Frideswide's, has been excavated in Christ Church.

Significantly, the site chosen for the early minster was beside the north–south Thames crossing on the line of the later St Aldates and Abingdon Road, a route important enough by the later eighth century to require considerable engineering work. Here indeed may be the 'oxen ford' from which the town is named, although some later evidence points to the ford at North Hinksey. It now seems likely that the earliest settlement called Oxford comprised a small lay community at the gates of St Frideswide's, flanking the important route from Mercia into Wessex, but firm archaeological confirmation is awaited.

Alfred, Edward the Elder and the Saxon *Burh*

We are told that on the death of Aethelred of Mercia in AD 911 the West Saxon king Edward the Elder, Alfred's son, took control of 'London and Oxford and the lands that belonged thereto'. By then Oxford was clearly an important place, and in the early tenth century, possibly earlier, it belonged to a system of fortified towns or *burhs* created as a defence against the Danes. The surviving rectilinear street plan, centred on Carfax, resembles that of other Saxon planned or 'planted' towns, and documents and archaeological evidence suggest strongly that the central streets of Oxford were deliberately laid out within a fortified enclosure at some date in the late tenth or early eleventh century. Instead of fortifying whatever settlement existed near St Frideswide's, the king provided land for an entirely new town. The building plots between the grid-plan of streets were no doubt quickly taken up by magnates, merchants and craftsmen, who saw the advantages of royal protection, strong military defences and a market located on an important trade route.

The area enclosed by the original earth banks and ramparts was smaller and squarer than the medieval walled town. The fortifications on the east were probably just west of Catte Street and Magpie Lane, on the west somewhere west of New Inn Hall Street and St Ebbe's Street, on the north on the line of the medieval wall, and on the south aligned with Brewer Street, meeting St Aldates near the south-west corner of Christ Church's Canterbury Quadrangle, the site of the medieval church of St Michael at Southgate. Churches seem to have been built at the other three principal gates: St Michael's church tower in Cornmarket Street,

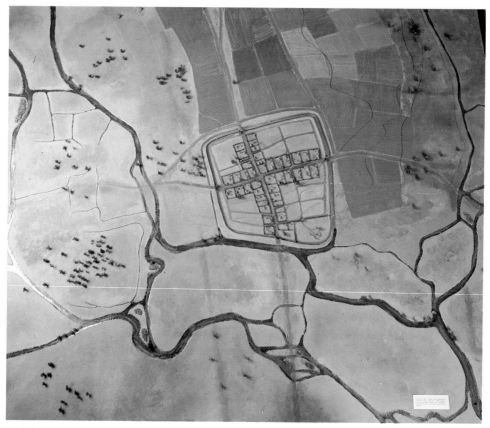

Model of Oxford as it may have looked in the tenth century. Later the Norman castle was built to the west and the walled area extended eastwards

Oxford's oldest building, marks the site of the north gate, and the original east and west gates were probably near St Mary's church in High Street and the demolished church of St Peter-le-Bailey at the west end of Queen Street.

The grid of central streets seems to have been established in a single operation, and under New Inn Hall Street, embedded in the original surface, was found a coin of Edward the Elder (d. AD 925), perhaps the safest indication of the date of the town's creation. Even so, Edward's father, King Alfred (d. AD 899), was the first to establish a system of fortified towns and he is associated with Oxford not only in legend but through a puzzling series of coins bearing his name and that of a mint called 'Orsnaforda' or 'Ohsnaforda'. Scholars are uncertain whether or not these coins were minted in Oxford, and in default of further evidence the identity of the king who founded Oxford must remain in doubt.

Late Saxon Oxford

As England became unified under Edward the Elder and his successors, Oxford ceased to be a border town in the military sense, but retained political and commercial significance because of its position between Wessex and Mercia. There was probably a royal residence in Oxford and certainly an important mint. In 1009 the town was sacked by the Danes under Thorkell the Tall in reprisal for a massacre of Danes in St Frideswide's church seven years earlier, and in 1013 Oxford submitted to Sweyn of Denmark. Despite its troubled history the town was a favoured meeting place for great royal councils, as in 1018 when Canute was accepted as ruler of England and in 1065 when Edward the Confessor was forced to negotiate with the rebels supporting Morcar.

By the time of the Norman Conquest Oxford was among the largest towns in England, with about a thousand houses and perhaps eleven churches. By then the original walled town had been extended, notably on the east to enclose suburban

The late Saxon tower of St Michael-at-the-Northgate church, with its 'long and short' stonework, is Oxford's oldest surviving stone building. It probably formed part of the town's defences in the eleventh century, and the church may have been built against it later

development between the town and the River Cherwell. The principal axis of the original town had been the established north–south route down St Aldate's to the Thames crossing, and although the street leading eastwards gave access to an important crossing of the Cherwell near Magdalen Bridge, it was not aligned on it. A curving road from the original east gate to the crossing became lined with houses, and when it was included in the extended late-Saxon defences a new gate was built near the surviving Eastgate Hotel. Thus was preserved the famous, aesthetically pleasing, bend in High Street, which was not part of the original rectilinear planned town.

Robert d'Oilly and the Castle

After the Norman Conquest the dominant figure in Oxford was Robert d'Oilly, a Norman adventurer who had fought at Hastings. In 1071 he built a huge castle on the west side of the town, destroying many houses. The line of the town walls was altered to integrate the castle in their circuit, but heavy fortifications were also maintained between castle and town, since d'Oilly clearly anticipated hostility

Painting of Castle mill beside St George's tower, by J.A. Shuffrey (1859–1939). The mill, Norman in origin, was demolished in the early twentieth century

from that side. The castle's great bailey was surrounded by a moat, fed from a branch of the Thames which also powered the castle mills, which later played an important part in the life of the town. Although the castle was largely destroyed in the seventeenth century there are impressive survivals, including the great motte or mound and St George's tower, part of a collegiate church founded by d'Oilly in 1074, but clearly constructed with defensive considerations in mind. Robert d'Oilly is also credited with improving the southern route out of Oxford by building the great causeway called Grandpont, a long series of stone arches, of which many survive under the modern Abingdon Road.

During the 'anarchy' of King Stephen's reign the castle was the scene of a famous event. In the winter of 1142, while the king was besieging the town, Queen Matilda escaped from the castle across the frozen Thames – dressed in white and unseen against the snow.

Twelfth-century limestone cresset lamp, found near Carfax. Oil was burned in the shallow bowl, or cresset, at the top. Usually such lamps were made of pottery

Late twelfth-century carved limestone base for a wooden cross, found in the nineteenth century in a buttress of the cathedral. Perhaps it once stood in the courtyard of St Frideswide's Priory, which preceded Christ Church on the site. The base was carved with Biblical scenes, and this shows Adam and Eve with the Tree of Knowledge

By courtesy of Christ Church

The Early Middle Ages

At first Oxford suffered under Norman rule, and the fact that Domesday Book, compiled twenty years after the Conquest, describing over half the town's properties as 'waste', suggests that there had been serious disruption of trade or some unrecorded disaster in addition to d'Oilly's castle works. By the twelfth century, however, the town was clearly recovering. Henry I built a royal residence, Beaumont Palace, outside the walls near the west end of the later Beaumont Street. Kings stayed there regularly, and Richard I and probably King John were born there.

The town's flourishing economy depended heavily on cloth and leather. Some of the wealthiest Jews in England lived in Oxford. Prosperity led to intensive building activity as the main streets, where the markets were held, became lined with narrow single-storey shops which were often leased separately from the larger dwelling houses behind, or the wide stone cellars below. Although stone and slates were not unknown, most houses were timber-framed and thatched, despite the risk of fires such as one in 1138 which was said to have burned the whole town. More parish churches were built and by the thirteenth century there were eighteen in the town and suburbs, plus at least one non-parochial chapel and St George's in the castle. Suburban expansion continued, particularly on the west in St Thomas's parish and on the north where the whole of St Giles Street was built up. An

This fine stretch of medieval town wall survives within the grounds of New College, and may be visited there. The foundations have been dated to about 1226

incomplete survey of 1279 listed some 1,100 houses and shops within and without the walls, implying a population well over 5,000.

A crucial development of the early Middle Ages was the establishment in Oxford of two important Augustinian monasteries, the refounded St Frideswide's in 1122 and Osney Abbey, built on an island west of the town in 1129, and in 1149 absorbing the college of secular canons at St George's. These institutions were to influence the development of the university.

Oxford's medieval religious houses were busy and prosperous. The beautiful encaustic floor tile and the gold and sapphire ring are from the site of Blackfriars, the *ampulla* (holy-water bottle for pilgrims) was found in Longwall Street, and the seal matrix near Donnington Bridge. The seal, showing a monk and the head of God, is inscribed 'Seal of Ralph of Sandwych', perhaps an abbot

The early medieval prick-spur was found in Queen Street, the two halves of medieval padlocks on the site of the Westgate Centre

This spout in the form of an angrily shouting person comes from a jug of the late thirteenth or fourteenth century found on the Blackfriars site in St Ebbes

The bone handle of a nineteenth-century wedding knife, inscribed LOVE, was found on the site of the Westgate Centre; the bone domino comes from the Blackfriars site, and the little die from the site of County Hall. The twelfth-century carved openwork fitting is of walrus ivory, probably imported from Scandinavia

Merchant Guild and Corporation

Even before the Conquest leading townspeople acted together as a group and 'all the burgesses of Oxford' held the great pasture, Port Meadow, in common. By the mid-twelfth century 'the citizens of Oxford of the commune of the city and of the guild merchant' were granting land and by 1191 they were using a communal seal. The powers and privileges of Oxford burgesses, modelled on those of London, were extended by various royal grants and in 1199 King John effectively freed townsmen from the control of royal reeves by granting them the borough in return for a fixed rent or 'fee farm'. Town government, based on the institutions of the guild merchant, was then free to develop independently, and during the thirteenth century the familiar form of corporate government through a mayor, bailiffs and aldermen, aided by a council, became established.

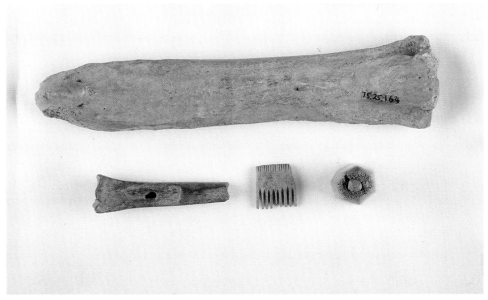

The bone ice-skate, worked from the long-bone of the horse, was tied to the shoes. The bone whistle, the comb (originally double-sided), and the chess pawn were all found in the St Ebbes area

The Beginnings of the University

There was no founder of the university. Oxford's geographical centrality and its comparative freedom from episcopal control (being on the border of Lincoln diocese) may have attracted scholarly clerics to the town, but the role of the monasteries and the secular canons of St George's was probably decisive. By the early twelfth century, individual scholars were lecturing to large audiences in Oxford and by c. 1200 there was evidently an organized *studium generale* or university, a loose association of scholars under a *magister scholarum*, following a curriculum similar to that of the university of Paris. Oxford quickly acquired a reputation as a centre of legal studies. By 1221 the university was headed by a chancellor, and thereafter, with massive royal, papal and episcopal support, its powers and privileges were steadily enlarged.

   The presence of the university attracted friars to Oxford, the Dominicans settling there in 1221, the Franciscans in 1224, the Carmelites in 1256, the Augustinians in 1267 and others later. About 1280, Cistercian monks founded Rewley Abbey as a *studium* for scholars of their order, and in 1284 the Benedictines established the first of their three colleges (Gloucester). The town was thus filled with monks and friars, in addition to the independent scholars who were of course all clerics. By 1300 there were perhaps 1,500 scholars in Oxford.

The Medieval Student

For most of the Middle Ages the university had almost no endowments and few buildings. Its principal meetings and ceremonies were held in the church of St Mary the Virgin where the 'congregation house' and a room above it for a library were begun in 1320, but most lecture halls and schools were in hired premises. Thus in the age of Robert Grosseteste, Roger Bacon and Duns Scotus, the unobservant traveller might pass through Oxford without noticing that there was a university at all. Three colleges, University, Balliol and Merton were founded in the thirteenth century, with several more in the later Middle Ages, but these housed only a small, privileged minority of mostly graduate fellows. Masters and scholars were scattered about in lodgings or academic halls. The practice of lodging with townsmen as 'chamber deacons' was increasingly discouraged and from 1410 all scholars were compelled to belong to a hall under the supervision of a principal.

The academic halls were ordinary (large) town houses rented by masters who provided both teaching and shelter for their pupils. Of the seventy or so academic halls rented in the mid-fifteenth century none survive unaltered, but Tackley's Inn (Nos 106-7 High Street) throws some light on the arrangements of the medieval student household. Shops on the street frontage and cellars below were leased separately from the academic hall which, approached by a passageway between the shops, comprised only a large open hall, two chambers, which might have been shared by ten scholars, and a kitchen in a separate building at the rear. The hall would have been used for lectures and meals, the chambers for sleeping and study. The ends of the chambers probably had small partitioned studies, each containing a desk and a book press.

Geoffrey Chaucer in 'The Miller's Tale' depicts the living conditions of a wealthy scholar, Nicholas, who lodged with a prosperous carpenter: his private chamber contained a bed, a shelf of books, musical and scientific instruments, a bow and arrow, food and drink, and much jewellery.

Town and Gown

The university brought prosperity to existing tradesmen and craftsmen, while attracting specialists such as scribes, bookbinders and parchmenters, many of whom were already settled in the Catte Street area by c. 1200. Conflict, however, was inevitable where two separately governed bodies with quite different priorities shared the same restricted space. Violence was commonplace in medieval student life, not only between scholars and townsmen, but also between northern and southern scholars. Town–gown riots were recorded regularly from the early thirteenth century, but the most notorious was on St Scholastica's Day (10 February) 1355. It began as a tavern brawl between scholars and the landlord of the Swindlestock at Carfax, and lasted for three days during which academic halls were sacked, a large mob of countrymen marched in to support the townsmen, and

Book production was one of Oxford's specialist industries from medieval times. Parchment sheets tended to curl unless held with clasps; the two shown came from Thames Street and the Greyfriars site. The bone parchment-pickers (above) had metal pins for puncturing the sheaf of sheets to rule uniform margins. Parchment books were costly, so lead *styli* (below) were also used to write on waxed wooden tablets

Some unusual personal ornaments from late medieval Oxford: the gold leaf ornaments may be from a belt; the cockerel mount is of copper alloy; the circular belt plate or brooch of gilded copper alloy is decorated with coloured enamel; the little hooked fastener has a face mask

six clerks were allegedly killed and many injured. Thereafter, until 1825, the mayor and burgesses were obliged to attend St Mary's church each year on St Scholastica's Day for a humiliating ceremony, which included handing over to the university 60 pence (one for each burgess of 1355). More important was that, after the riot of 1355, the university won confirmation and enlargement of all the powers and privileges which it had already obtained through royal intervention in previous disputes.

The outcome of these successive agreements and royal charters was that the university not only gained exclusive control of its own members and their dependent servants, but also of many aspects of the town's government such as the market, the supervision of the streets, the pricing and inspection of ale, bread and other products, and much of the policing of the town. Although for centuries townsmen strove continually to regain control, they made little progress until the nineteenth century.

The Later Middle Ages

The university's growth to some extent masked the town's economic decline, which was particularly severe after the Black Death of 1349, but probably started much earlier when Oxford began to lose its important cloth industry to rural entrepreneurs. Other factors contributed, not least a changing pattern of road communications to London, and the decline of Thames navigation which left the town somewhat isolated. Acquisition of much town property by religious houses effectively removed capital assets from townsmen, and the important wine trade suffered with the outbreak of the Hundred Years' War. The Black Death, which wiped out perhaps a third of Oxford's population and many of its leading men, was therefore all the more catastrophic. The town's tradesmen became increasingly dependent on the university.

In the later Middle Ages the suburbs contracted and there was much decay within the walls, allowing the university to start the expansion which culminated in its physical dominance of much of the eastern side of the town. Land containing fifty-one vacant plots in the south-east corner of the town, a haunt of undesirable characters, was acquired by William of Wykeham for the foundation of New College in 1379. Merton College similarly acquired much of the land between Merton Street and the town wall, and even in the central streets The Queen's College, University, Oriel, All Souls, Lincoln and Exeter all absorbed many former house sites in the later Middle Ages. In 1427 the university started work on its first major building, the Divinity School and library. The scale of college building changed as large stone buildings and high-walled enclosures became predominant. Following the example of New College, most later colleges arranged their chief buildings around spacious quadrangles. The organization of the university began to change as academic halls declined and colleges took over the teaching of undergraduates. By 1552 there were thirteen colleges and only eight halls, which had expanded to resemble miniature colleges.

Renaissance and Reformation

Humanist ideas began to influence the university in the late Middle Ages. Erasmus and Thomas More were in Oxford in the 1490s. When Henry VIII dissolved the monasteries and friaries much of the Oxford property of local religious houses passed sooner or later to colleges. The most notable beneficiary was Christ Church, which was built by Cardinal Wolsey on the site of St Frideswide's, and whose rich endowments included the former possessions of Osney Abbey. In some other respects, however, the Reformation provoked a temporary decline in the university. The stream of undergraduates seconded from religious houses dried up, and numbers were further reduced when Henry VIII abolished the study of canon law. There was an understandable hesitancy over attending university in an age when ideas were dangerous. In the 1550s the Protestant martyrs Cranmer, Latimer and Ridley, all Cambridge men, were brought to trial in the more conservative Oxford, and burned to death in the city ditch (later Broad Street). In that period the

'Real', or Royal, tennis being played at Merton College. The Merton court, rebuilt in 1798, is the oldest such court still in use in England, except for that at Hampton Court
Photograph courtesy of Oxford Archaeological Unit

Seventeenth-century tennis balls from Wadham College, one of several colleges with 'real' tennis courts in the sixteenth and seventeenth centuries

19

A recreated Elizabethan inn parlour, based on that of John Tattleton (d. 1581), who kept a tavern (including the surviving 'Painted Room') at 3 Cornmarket Street. There is a fragment of original painted plaster, a sixteenth-century oak table and stool from Trinity College, and sixteenth- and seventeenth-century pottery from the site of the Westgate Centre

Museum of Oxford

university's numbers reached an all-time low, its library was dispersed, and there was even a decision to sell the bookshelves. The citizens, heavily dependent on the university, suffered accordingly.

The Great Rebuilding

Queen Elizabeth I's reign restored political and religious stability, and over the next hundred years both city and university were transformed. The demand for well-educated clergy, lawyers and schoolmasters, and a recognition among the

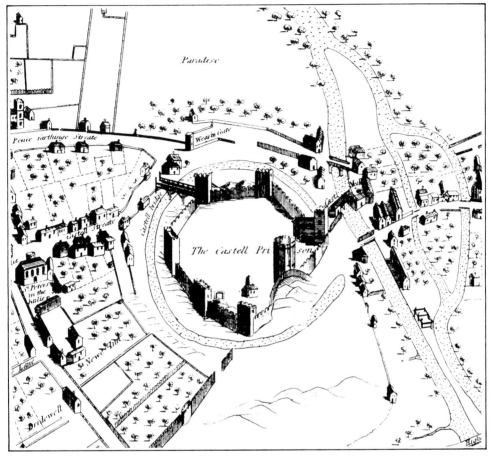

Oxford castle in 1578, from the map by Ralph Agas (note that North is at the bottom). The shell keep on the mound, St George's tower and church, Shire hall, other stone wall-towers, and Castle mill are all shown intact

social élite that academic education should form part of a gentleman's training led to a sharp increase in university recruitment. Even aristocratic sons were encouraged to spend time at the university, and Oxford's citizens provided tennis courts, fencing and dancing schools, and other recreations for the idle men of fashion.

The university's expansion was the dominant factor in the city's revival. Oxford had acquired city status when the diocese of Oxford, with its cathedral at Christ Church, was created in 1542. Its population at that time was probably only about 3,000, but by the 1630s it had more than trebled to around 10,000,

Drawing by J.A. Shuffrey (1859–1939) of a surviving house at the corner of Rose Place and St Aldates, showing carved brackets

and in the 1660s was much the same, including over 2,000 members of the university.

Intensive building activity changed the spacious walled city, depicted by Ralph Agas in 1578, into the crowded, overspilling city mapped by David Loggan in 1675. Jesus College was built soon after Agas's map was drawn, and although only two colleges, Wadham (1610) and Pembroke (1624), were founded in the seventeenth century, it was one of the greatest periods of university building. The monastic colleges taken over by Trinity (1555), St John's (1557), and Gloucester Hall (1560), later Worcester College, were not much altered until the seventeenth century, when nearly all the other established colleges were greatly extended by the addition of attic storeys or the construction of large new quadrangles. University buildings began to dominate the central area: the great Schools Quadrangle and other additions were built at the Bodleian Library, and close by were the Sheldonian Theatre (1664–9), used for university ceremonies and to house the printing press, and the Old Ashmolean Museum (1678–83). The Botanic (earlier the Physic) Garden, given to the university by the Earl of Danby, mostly dates from the 1630s.

The loss of house sites to the expanding university and colleges, and the need to provide for a rapidly growing population was met by infilling, subdivision, large-scale rebuilding and the development of new sites. The central streets became lined with three- and four-storey houses, and the long plots behind street frontages were built up. Vacant areas of 'waste' belonging to the city on both sides

The original sixteenth-century wooden quarterboys from St Martin's church, Carfax. The clock, with replica quarterboys, was moved to its present position on the church tower when the body of the church was demolished in 1896
Drawing by Edith Gollnast

of the city wall and ditch were now developed, particularly the Holywell, Broad Street, Ship Street, St Michael's Street and George Street areas, and housing expanded into Gloucester Green.

Timber-framed construction continued to be popular, perhaps because it allowed ostentatious fronts with pargetting, bargeboards and carved brackets. Good examples survive at Kemp Hall (1637), behind No. 130 High Street, and No. 126 High Street (refronted late seventeenth century), both built by Oxford aldermen. Stone houses tended to be built on larger sites away from the central area, for instance Postmaster's Hall in Merton Street and Kettell Hall in Broad Street. The great courtyard inns expanded, taking up much of the space in the central streets. The Mitre and the former Golden Cross are notable examples. By the sixteenth century the city was already regarded as beautiful, and by the eighteenth century, when it had been enriched by monumental buildings, it was described as 'the delight and ornament of the kingdom, not to say of the world'.

The city's economy remained largely dependent on the university, although Oxford was famous in this period for its glovers and cutlers who served a wider market. The wealthy and most powerful citizens tended to be large shopkeepers (such as mercers and drapers), brewers and innkeepers. Their prosperity and confidence was reflected not only in their houses, but also in civic life, where great efforts were made to provide public services, improve public health and make proper provision for the poor. The corporation, representing the large and proud body of freemen, achieved full constitutional development with a royal charter in 1605, and carried on a vigorous and unremitting power struggle with the university throughout the period.

Only a small proportion of Oxford college gold and silver plate survived the Royalist occupation of 1642–6. The replicas seen here include examples from The Queen's College, Corpus Christi, New College, and All Souls, on loan from The Victoria and Albert Museum

The Civil War

The Civil War brought a sudden interruption to the growth of both city and university, and again highlighted their differences. From 1642 to 1646 Oxford was the capital of Royalist England and headquarters of the king's army. Charles I took over the city and university, exploiting their resources to finance military campaigns. The king lodged at Christ Church and the queen, Henrietta Maria, at Merton College.

Three houses in St Aldates, where, according to a census of 1644, six Royalist soldiers were billeted

When it came to taking sides in the war there was no straight town–gown division, but in general the university supported the king, while several leading townsmen fled to Abingdon when the Royalists arrived. Most citizens kept a low profile, and many benefited from the presence of the court. Silver plate from the colleges was turned into coins by the mint at New Inn Hall; gunpowder was made at Osney; munitions were stored in New College cloisters; and captured Parliamentarians were imprisoned in the castle. Elaborate defensive earthworks were thrown up around the city, destroying property particularly in the St Clement's area. The most serious destruction during the Civil War, however, was an accidental fire in 1644, which swept the area between George Street and St Ebbe's.

By 1646 the war was over and Oxford surrendered to a Parliamentary army on 24 June, the king having escaped in disguise two months previously. In 1651 the military authorities ordered that the city's defences, including the castle, should be slighted. Loggan's map of 1675 shows that the castle had been reduced to little more than the mound, a ruined court house, and St George's tower, while few of the Civil War earthworks are visible, except on the north.

After the war, the city council, to which exiled Parliamentarians had been restored, expected to win back some of the powers lost to the now slightly discredited university. The university, however, was still influential enough to acquire Oliver Cromwell as chancellor, and made no important concessions before it again seized the initiative on the restoration of Charles II in 1660. The university's contribution to intellectual life during the Interregnum was notable, for it was then that a group of mathematicians and scientists, including Robert Boyle and Christopher Wren, began to meet at Wadham College, forming the nucleus of what was to become the Royal Society.

Three bottles of the late seventeenth and eighteenth centuries, found in Oxford. Left and middle: eighteenth-century gin bottles, for the cheap and popular Dutch gin; right: late seventeenth-century port wine bottle

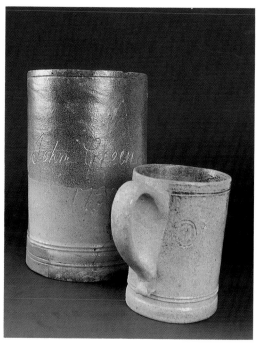

Eighteenth-century stoneware ale tankards from the site of the Westgate Centre. The one on the left bears the owner's name, 'John Green, 1730'

The Election in the Guildhall by Egbert van Heemskerk. This propaganda picture records James II's attempt to force Oxford City Council to choose his nominee as alderman on 14 March 1688. By December, James had lost the throne to William of Orange

By courtesy of Oxford City Council

The Later Seventeenth Century

After the Restoration numbers in both university and city temporarily returned to pre-war levels. The development of scientific studies, and the opening of the printing press and the museum reflected a new vigour in the university, while the Oxford depicted by Anthony Wood was clearly a lively university and county town. From the 1670s, however, recruitment into the university began to decline. Academic education lost some of its prestige among the aristocracy and became more expensive for others. It was even doubted whether the university could provide an appropriate education for the sons of the serious-minded gentry: some

A knucklebone house floor of *c*. 1700, excavated in Park End Street; it is made of ox bones set in mortar

Eighteenth-century hand-operated fire engine from Christ Church

*By courtesy of the Museum of the
History of Science, Oxford*

feared that it might encourage subversive ideas, and one late seventeenth-century mayor described it as 'a debauched place, a rude place, a place of no discipline'.

The university's troubles and the levelling off of national population growth ended Oxford's expansion. Its economy became more inward-looking as the cutlery and gloving industries declined. Party politics, the clash between Whigs and Tories so hotly debated in Oxford's proliferating coffee-houses, began to influence town–gown disputes, as in 1683 when there was a violent riot between townsmen supporting the Duke of Monmouth and scholars favouring the Duke of York. Crown interference with the corporation for political and religious reasons (frequently with enthusiastic university support) led to the exclusion of influential citizens, while entry to the freedom of the city began to be manipulated by political patrons. The period between the Restoration and the Revolution of 1688 saw the beginnings of a process which reduced the once proud corporation to an ineffectual and ill-funded institution, almost a private club, and no longer truly representative of the city community.

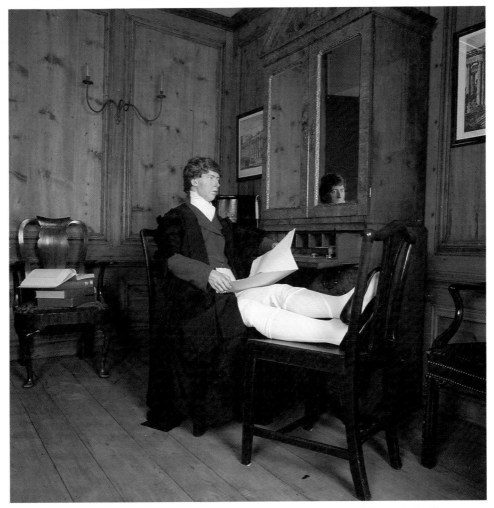

Reconstruction of an undergraduate's room in Christ Church in the 1770s. Most sets of college rooms comprised a panelled study and bedroom. The gown was made to an original pattern by Shepherd & Woodward of Oxford for the Museum of Oxford

The University in Decline

The university, portrayed by its enemies as Jacobite, obstinately clerical, and steeped in port-wine and prejudice, was for much of the eighteenth century on the defensive and in decline. The Industrial Revolution in Britain and the intellectual

29

revolution of the European Enlightenment passed Oxford by; the university was content to function as the guardian of religious orthodoxy, while offering the future clergy of the Church of England a traditional Classical education. Men such as John Wesley, Edmond Halley and William Blackstone ensured that the university was never totally moribund, but Oxford's tarnished reputation led to a decline in entrants from 450 a year in the 1650s to as few as 200 a century later.

However, in one area, architecture, the university excelled. Oxford continued to be embellished with fine buildings such as the Clarendon Building (completed 1715), the Radcliffe Camera (1748) and the Radcliffe Observatory (1794); one college (Queen's) was completely rebuilt, and twelve of the other eighteen altered. The enormous expenditure was designed at least in part to encourage the return of those who had been frightened off by the university's reputation.

The Eighteenth-Century City

Oxford's citizens, benefiting economically from the small but lavish academic community and from the unceasing building activity, were now content to live peacefully and profitably with their former adversaries. In 1721 it was noted that 'Oxford daily increases in fine clothes and fine buildings, never were bricklayers, carpenters, tailors, and periwig-makers better encouraged there'. Demand from the university for luxury goods encouraged increasing numbers of jewellers,

Three panels of a 'Dance of Death' wall painting, probably copied from sixteenth-century originals in the late eighteenth century. They show death dancing with a lawyer, a canon and a physician. The panels once decorated the hall of the antiquarian Alderman William Fletcher, who lived at 46 Broad Street between 1787 and 1826

TO THE RIGHT HONOURABLE LORD GRENVILLE,

CHANCELLOR OF THE UNIVERSITY OF OXFORD, &c. &c. &c.

This PLATE representing the ASCENT of Mr SADLER, the celebrated BRITISH AERONAUT, at OXFORD, at the COMMEMORATION July 1810, Is most respectfully dedicated by his Lordship's most obedient humble Servant

C. M. Jones.

Tinted engraving of the ascent of the balloonist James Sadler over Oxford on 7 July 1810. Sadler is famous as Britain's first aeronaut; his tombstone may be seen in the churchyard of St Peter-in-the-East, now part of St Edmund Hall

gunsmiths, and makers of clocks, watches and scientific instruments.

The city remained undisturbed by the Industrial Revolution, even after the opening of the Oxford Canal in 1790 brought cheap coal and made Oxford briefly the centre of water-borne trade between London and the Midlands. Although a market centre, Oxford's regional importance was restricted by the influence of Banbury to the north, and Abingdon and Reading to the south. The shopkeepers and craftsmen of Oxford, concerned to keep out competitors, and as freemen controlling trade through the city council, were content to leave things as they were. Those who would have welcomed greater opportunity, the 'operative and working classes', remained at the mercy of the university vacations when the colleges emptied.

Politically the freemen were controlled by local magnates, the earls of Abingdon and the dukes of Marlborough, who, in return for the election of their candidates to Parliament, agreed to meet the corporation's burgeoning debts. Oxford elections were corrupt even by the standards of the day, but the mark was overstepped in 1766 when the city's seats were virtually put up for sale to the highest bidder. The city fathers, reprimanded at the Bar of the House of Commons and sent to Newgate prison for five days, were chastened but incorrigible.

The Age of Improvement

From the later eighteenth century improvements were made. In the university the introduction of an honours degree, written examinations, competitive college fellowships and improved teaching pointed the way to the radical reforms of the Victorian age. For the city the year 1771 marked a watershed: the Paving Commission, which was to transform Oxford constitutionally and physically, was set up, and the city's eleven parishes were united under a Board of Poor Law Guardians which built a new workhouse on Rats and Mice Hill, later Wellington Square. The Paving Commission, one of the first in the country and created on the university's initiative, placed the administration of the city in the hands of a joint body of citizens and academics, leaving the corporation, although represented on the commission, with only a peripheral role.

The commissioners' improvements marked the end of medieval Oxford. The rebuilding of Magdalen Bridge and the removal of the north and east gates, and of Carfax conduit, allowed traffic easier access to the city centre, an achievement little appreciated by later generations. Street markets were transferred to a new covered market; myriad stalls, pumps, shop signs and obstructions were swept away, and the city was newly paved, lighted and drained. The 'rage' of improvement, by no means limited to the commissioners, had begun in 1769 with the making of New Road through the former castle bailey, and it continued with the rebuilding of Folly Bridge and the demolition of St Clement's church, which stood at what is now The

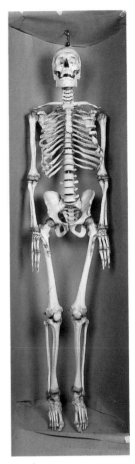

Left Crime and punishment in eighteenth-century Oxford. The deposition of Richard Kilby, implicating Giles Covington in the murder of a pedlar in Nuneham Woods in 1789. Kilby was pardoned, but Covington and two other men were hanged for the crime. *Right* The skeleton of Giles Covington. His body was cut down from the gallows at Oxford prison, dissected at Christ Church anatomy school, and subsequently became an anatomical specimen

By courtesy of The University Museum, Oxford

Plain, east of Magdalen Bridge. The Oxford canal was brought into the city along the eastern edge of Port Meadow to terminate at New Road wharves, later the site of Nuffield College. The Thames Navigation Commissioners, not to be outdone, removed weirs that had long impeded river traffic.

It seemed in 1836 that progress would be crowned by the arrival in Oxford of the Great Western Railway, despite opposition from the university, worried about student discipline, and from city tradesmen, fearful of London shops. The

Push-cart from Wigmore's Walton Manor Dairies in 1897

Model river barge, possibly made by George Davis, a Shillingford bargemaster. The model bears the registration number One, and dates from after the Registration Act of 1879. After the completion of the Oxford canal in 1790, coal and building materials from the Midlands were brought to the Thames valley by water. Narrow river barges were constructed to travel both on river and canal

Magdalen Bridge and Magdalen College Tower in 1880

Pencil sketch of Folly Bridge on the Thames by William Turner, Oxford's outstanding landscape artist. Working in the early nineteenth century in watercolours, oils and pencil, Turner portrayed romantic views of the local landscape

proposal foundered on the refusal of local landowners to sell, and when the railway eventually came, in 1844, it was a branch line from Didcot. An LNWR line from Bletchley, opened in 1851, gave Oxford slightly more significance in the national railway network.

The City Expands

Oxford's population increased fourfold between 1801 (11,921) and 1901 (49,285), the most rapid growth (50 per cent) occurring in the three decades to 1831. The town grew enormously, spreading on to the low-lying river floodplains. Rows of cheap houses spread south and west of the city centre, in St Ebbe's, St Thomas's and Jericho, built typically for college servants and for workers employed at the

High Street *c.* 1900, with Brasenose College in the foreground. Several college servants can be seen on the right

Reconstruction of the kitchen of a terraced house in Cardigan Street, Jericho, in the late 1880s. The kitchen served as a living room for the family – it was used for eating, sitting in, working (many women 'took in' college laundry) and bathing, as well as for preparing food

Museum of Oxford

wharves, on the railway, at the University Press, the gasworks or the breweries. Those areas were the worst affected by the epidemics that periodically swept the city.

Apart from Beaumont Street, laid out from the 1820s, there was little new housing for the better-off until the development of exclusive estates at Park Town and Norham Manor from the 1850s. The decision of St John's College to permit controlled development of its land there and further north led to the creation of the celebrated suburb of North Oxford, favoured home of the successful tradesman and professional, of the university professor and college head, and, after marriage was permitted in 1877, the don. Occupying a social status between that of North Oxford and the poorer suburbs were the new developments along Cowley, Iffley, Abingdon and Botley Roads. Some of the most rapid growth took place in St Clement's and Headington, brought within the city boundary in 1837.

Economic Life

The Municipal Corporations Act of 1835 abolished trading restrictions, and the consequent rush for university business was a reason for the city's continued growth. To outsiders Oxford seemed fairly affluent, but its economy was still narrowly based on the provision of goods and services. Although the growing population gave tradesmen some independence, university custom remained the

Webber's, once the City Drapery Stores, had its premises at 10–14 High Street. From the late nineteenth century it expanded and diversified into a department store

Elliston & Cavell was Oxford's largest department store. Established as a drapery in 1835, its premises in Magdalen Street were extended and rebuilt in the late nineteenth century and early twentieth. In 1953 it became part of the Debenhams Group, losing the name Elliston & Cavell in 1973

Workers in Cooper's marmalade factory, Park End Street, *c.* 1900. The building still stands near the railway station. Unskilled factory work was a common female occupation

likeliest route to prosperity. The town's contrasting shopping areas emphasized the point: Queen Street and St Ebbe's catered for the cheaper end of the market on a cash-only basis, whereas the more fashionable establishments of High Street, Cornmarket and Broad Street offered more expensive goods on long-term credit. Members of the university might be allowed two years to settle their acounts, and the archives of the vice-chancellor's court contain plentiful evidence of those, like Oscar Wilde, who defaulted. As a result, Oxford prices were always higher than elsewhere. Some of the best-known shops were among the town's leading employers: the famous 'Spiers of Oxford' (R.J. Spiers & Son of 102–3 High Street), sellers of stationery, china and glass, employed thirty people in 1851. Spiers & Son did not survive the nineteenth century, but other Oxford establishments of the period, their fame travelling with generations of graduates, flourished into the twentieth: Elliston & Cavell of Magdalen Street, drapers, and Grimbly Hughes of Cornmarket Street, grocers, both taken over by large chains in the 1950s; Frank and Jane Cooper of High Street, whose marmalade was so popular that in 1900 a factory was built for its manufacture in Park End Street.

Oxford's greatest economic problem was underemployment, its cause the university vacations. The railway, when it eventually came, brought fewer new jobs than had been hoped for, and even they were offset by the collapse of the coaching trade that followed. The great coaching inns, the Angel (later replaced by the university Examination Schools) and the Star (demolished for Woolworth's) were bankrupted. Apart from the University Press, the only industries of any note were the railway, Lucy's Ironworks, the breweries and two clothing factories. It was significant that in 1851, 27 per cent of the total employed population was engaged in domestic service, compared to the national average of 13 per cent. Many were men working for colleges, but colleges employed fewer than a fifth of the 3,450 domestic servants who in Oxford were cheap as well as plentiful. More than a quarter of the employed population was still engaged in domestic service in 1901.

The university failed to match the city's growth in the first half of the nineteenth century and comprised only 5 or 6 per cent of the total in 1861, compared to 10 per cent in 1801. The city, not surprisingly, stagnated, but was pulled along later in the century as the university began a rapid expansion. The university building boom, which continued for much of the nineteenth century, kept the building trades buoyant, as did suburban expansion. A major new development was the movement of large numbers of students into lodgings when licensing began in 1868. The opportunity was eagerly seized on and by 1879 there were no fewer than 580 licensed houses, accommodating some 1,000 students. The growth of tourism from the late nineteenth century provided a further boost, and the city also benefited from Oxford's development as a residential centre as North Oxford expanded. Nevertheless, Oxford was reckoned a 'poor place for the industrial population', and the city's MP, the brewer A.W. Hall, declared in 1890 that 'the great need of Oxford is some large industry'.

St Aldates in 1907, looking north from Folly Bridge. Tramlines can be seen in the foreground

Cornmarket Street in 1907, by Oxford photographer Henry Taunt, showing a horse-drawn tram, small horse-drawn vehicles and cyclists

Riots and Revels

Social life revolved around the university until, in the later nineteenth century, townspeople began increasingly to organize their own societies, sports and entertainments. University events and celebrations such as Eights Week and the May Day ceremony at Magdalen College tower were shared by townspeople, whose own great festivals were the autumn fairs held in St Giles's and St Clement's. Those other famous occasions on which the two came together, in town–gown riots, often gave the impression of being more sport than war, although there were one or two serious outbreaks in the nineteenth century, the last and greatest during bread riots in 1867. Celebrations on 5 November, the traditional occasion for battle, were tamed by the combined efforts of the university and city authorities, and by the growth of alternative, more socially acceptable, outlets for youthful energies. Guy Fawkes Night rowdyism largely died away after the Second World War.

The Victorian University

The university changed beyond recognition during the nineteenth century as the old clerical society was gradually dismantled and replaced by a more recognizably modern institution devoted to teaching and scholarship. For a time the university seemed to be tearing itself apart when, in the wake of the Tractarian controversy, John Henry Newman had in 1845 converted to Roman Catholicism, leaving the university open to the charge that it was no longer competent even to defend the Church of England. Reforms were eventually imposed by parliamentary commission in the 1850s and 1870s, and carried through by influential figures such as Henry Liddell (better known to most people today as the father of Alice) at Christ Church, Mark Pattison at Lincoln College and the best known of all, Benjamin Jowett at Balliol College.

For the first time it was possible to think in terms of an academic career at Oxford. The teaching of science, in particular, was urgently promoted as people became aware of the extent to which Germany had forged ahead of Britain. The university therefore inevitably retrieved much of the ground it had lost since the late Middle Ages to the all-powerful colleges: science has to be organized on a university-wide basis. Thus, although there is a Science Area in Oxford, there is no corresponding Arts Area, and the teaching of the humanities has continued to be organized by the colleges.

An Association for the Higher Education of Women at Oxford was established in 1878 and the first two women's colleges, Lady Margaret Hall and Somerville, opened in 1879. St Hugh's (1886) and St Hilda's (1893) followed. The hostility encountered by the women accounts for the formidable reputation of those early colleges, their principals aware that the merest breath of scandal would be seized upon by triumphant enemies. Although the women sat university exams, they were not formally awarded degrees until 1920.

Park End Street under water, by the Oxford photographer Henry Taunt in 1875. For much of Oxford's history the areas south and west of the city centre were subject to severe flooding. Careful management has reduced the risk in modern times

St Giles's fair in 1895. The fair developed from the parish wake during the eighteenth century, and in the nineteenth became a major event for the whole county. It was primarily a pleasure fair, always held on the Monday and Tuesday following the first Sunday after St Giles's day (1 September)

Fairground model of the 'smallest show on earth', one of a series of models by Neville Rainsley of Oxford made in the 1930s and 1940s. Rainsley displayed his working models to the public at St Giles's fair

By courtesy of Executors of Mrs Neville Rainsley

From the mid-nineteenth century, as increasing numbers of students entered the reformed university, a sustained period of college building began. Most colleges undertook some building work and one or two, such as Balliol and Exeter, were rebuilt almost completely. New colleges were founded: Keble in 1868, and, following the removal of religious tests in 1871, Mansfield (Congregationalist) in 1886 and Manchester (non-denominational) in 1889. Neo-Gothic was the predominant architectural style. The university, too, undertook some major projects, notably the Ashmolean Museum (opened 1845), the University Museum (1860) and the Examination Schools in High Street (1882).

The Reform of Local Government

Oxford's growth put great strain on the old system of local government through a variety of sometimes competing bodies. The most important body was the Oxford Local Board, which replaced the Paving Commission in 1865. City and university each had its own police force, the former patrolling by day, the latter by night, until in 1869 a single force was set up on Home Office instructions. The vice-chancellor's court retained civil and criminal jurisdiction, in cases where one party was a member of the university, into the later twentieth century. Many of the anomalies

Keble College, designed by William Butterfield, was built between 1868 and 1882. The college was a new foundation commemorating John Keble, a founder of the High Church Oxford Movement in the 1830s. The first college to be built in brick, it was highly controversial

Cardinal J.H. Newman (1801–90), who, with John Keble, was one of the founders of the Oxford Movement. Newman was vicar of the university church of St Mary the Virgin from 1828 to 1841, when he retired because of controversy over his religious ideas

were resolved in 1889 when Oxford became a county borough and the university was given representation on a strengthened corporation. The new town hall and public library (now the Museum of Oxford), opened in 1896, were a public expression of pride in Oxford's new status. Separate university representation on the city council was ended in 1974.

The Balance Tilts

The 'large industry' for which Oxford had looked without hope in the nineteenth century appeared unexpectedly in the twentieth, the result of the outstanding success of a local man, William Morris, later Lord Nuffield. He made his first bicycle in 1892, his first motor car in 1912. In 1913 he transferred his business from the centre of Oxford to the former Military Training College at Cowley, where he employed 300 men; in 1938 he employed 10,000. His success attracted other industries and in 1926 the Pressed Steel Company, soon to outgrow Morris Motors, was established at Cowley to supply car bodies. The rapid growth of the motor industry freed the city at last from economic dependence on the university, but at the cost of reliance upon the motor car. The impact of industrialization overturned the old job hierarchy as colleges were forced for the first time to compete for labour. In 1936 Oxford was, with Coventry and Luton, the most prosperous town in England, but rapid population growth in the 1920s and '30s, fuelled by immigration, inevitably created strains, both socially and upon the region's infrastructure. Some eight thousand new houses were built, mostly by private developers, as formerly separate villages around Oxford such as Cowley, Marston, Headington, Iffley, Hinksey and Wolvercote were absorbed. By 1938 the population living east of the River Cherwell had outstripped that of the old city to the west.

The decline of the motor industry in the later twentieth century has presented problems, but a combination of new and traditional employment has eased the transformation. The nature of much of that employment emphasizes the resurgence of the university as a major influence on the city's economic life, albeit indirectly. Oxford has become Britain's chief publishing centre outside London and it houses one of the largest medical research complexes in Europe. It remains one of the country's great tourist attractions.

The Modern University

The university's reputation today is as high as it has ever been. It benefited greatly from the philanthropy of Lord Nuffield, who not only founded in 1937 the college that bears his name, but also gave enormous sums of money for medical and scientific research. The twentieth century has been remarkable for the number of postgraduate colleges and institutions created. Apart from Nuffield they have included St Antony's College (1950), Linacre College (1962), Wolfson College (1966) and Green College (1979). One new undergraduate college, St Peter's (1961), was wholly a twentieth-century foundation; while the others, St Anne's (1952) and St Catherine's (1963), originated as nineteenth-century societies for non-collegiate students. In 1991 there were thirty-five colleges plus six permanent private halls founded by various religious denominations, providing for approximately 10,000 undergraduates and 4,000 postgraduates. In 1974 some colleges became co-educational, and by 1991 only two, the women's colleges of St Hilda's and St Hugh's, remained single sex. A further 9,000 students attended Oxford Polytechnic at Headington. Founded in 1955 as the Oxford College of Technology, polytechnic status was acquired in 1970, and the institution has since achieved

Workers on the final assembly of Bullnose Morris cars in the 1920s. William Morris transformed Oxford's economy. He pioneered the cheap, mass-production of cars from parts obtained from outside suppliers and assembled on production lines, with each gang of workers performing a specific task

In the 1930s houses were built at Florence Park, Cowley, to provide cheap accommodation for families who had left depressed areas like South Wales and the North East. Most worked at Morris Motors, Pressed Steel, or Osberton Radiators. Eight thousand new houses were built in Oxford during the 1920s and 1930s, many of them in Cowley

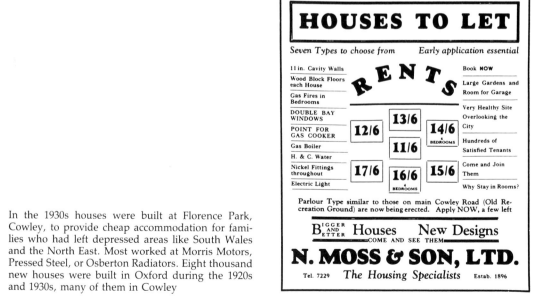

Model of 1948 showing proposed new scheme for Oxford city centre. The inner ring road bisecting Christ Church Meadow was abandoned in the face of local opposition, but St Ebbe's was cleared for redevelopment in the 1960s

international repute. The present-day Oxford undergraduate, living for at least part of the time in lodgings in town, worrying about rent and prices, is not unlike the medieval student. In one respect, of course, the modern student resembles *her* predecessors not at all.

The Modern City

The creation in 1956 of the Oxford green belt, the first outside London, has checked haphazard development around the city, but the decision to channel growth elsewhere in the county created the problem of commuters. Planning policy has swung between aiming to restrict traffic and trying to ease its flow. A large part of St Ebbe's was cleared in the 1960s for roads and car parks, the population being rehoused on a huge new estate south of the city at Blackbird Leys. An inner relief road across Christ Church Meadow, planned to follow the clearances, was eventually abandoned and St Ebbe's has since been largely rebuilt. The emphasis is now much more on attempting to limit the number of private vehicles coming into the city. Park-and-ride car parks around the ring road have helped to reduce congestion, but schemes for street closures and strict traffic control have not won general acceptance.

Oxford's Changing Face

The celebrated golden glow of Oxford's buildings has recently been restored by a massive cleaning and restoration programme that began with the establishment of the Oxford Historic Buildings Fund in 1957. Oxford's blackened and crumbling appearance at that time gave rise to the popular story of the tourist peering through a window with the exclamation 'These ruins are inhabited!'. Conservation of Oxford's historic centre was for long limited to college and university buildings and, despite the protests of a few, town buildings were destroyed that elsewhere would have been cherished. The city's conservation officer and groups of concerned citizens, notably through the Oxford Preservation Trust and the Oxford Civic Society, have gradually shifted public attitudes. There have been successes, both in the quality of new architecture, as in part of St Ebbe's and some college buildings, and in the restoration and conversion of old buildings, as at the Golden Cross Yard and the former Ship Inn (a Laura Ashley shop in 1991) in Cornmarket Street.

Oxford Tomorrow

For most people the word 'Oxford' is synonymous with the few crammed acres that provide the theme of guidebook, novel, poem and film. Oxford belongs to the world, and there are times when the world seems to be beating a path to its door. The city, however, is more than a precious concentration of buildings. It is also a working university city, an industrial, commercial and administrative centre. The struggle to reconcile its various functions remains unresolved, and Oxford is still perhaps uncertain what kind of city it should be. The study of its history at least provides some understanding of this extraordinary place, enabling more trustworthy planning for its second millennium.